PRESIDENTS OF THE U.S.A.

JAMES K. POLK
OUR ELEVENTH PRESIDENT

by Ann Graham Gaines

THE CHILD'S WORLD ®

Published in the United States of America

The Child's World®
1980 Lookout Drive • Mankato, MN 56003-1705
800-599-READ • www.childsworld.com

Acknowledgments
The Child's World®: Mary Berendes, Publishing Director

The Creative Spark: Mary McGavic, Project Director and Page Production;
Shari Joffe, Editorial Director; Deborah Goodsite, Photo Research

The Design Lab: Kathleen Petelinsek, Design

Content Advisers: John Holtzapple, Director; and Tom Price, Curator; James K.
Polk Ancestral Home, Columbia, Tennessee

Photos
Cover and page 3: White House Historical Association (White House Collection),
(detail); White House Historical Association (White House Collection)

Interior: Alamy: 5 (Jon Arnold Images Ltd), 35 and 39 (North Wind Picture
Archives); The Art Archive: 29 (National Portrait Gallery Washington);
Cincinnati Art Museum: 20 (Gift of Charles H. Kellogg Jr. Accession
#1890.54); Courtesy George Eastman House: 33; Corbis: 4 (The Corcoran
Gallery of Art), 10 (Peter Harholdt), 23 (David J. & Janice L. Frent Collection),
25 (Craig Tuttle); The Granger Collection, New York: 6-7, 8, 18, 19, 22
and 38, 28 30, 31, 37; The Hermitage: Home of President Andrew Jackson.
Nashville, TN: 16; The Image Works: 27 (Scherl/SV-Bilderdienst), 36 (U.S.
National Archives/Roger-Viollet); iStockphoto: 44 (Tim Fan); The James K.
Polk Ancestral Home, Columbia, Tennessee: 12, 13, 14, 31; Kevin Davidson
Illustration: 24, 34; Picture History: 26; SuperStock: 17 and 39 (Huntington
Library); Courtesy of the Tennessee State Museum: 21; University of North
Carolina Library at Chapel Hill: 9 (North Carolina Collection), 15 (Dialectic
and Philanthropic Society); U.S. Air Force photo: 45; White House Historical
Association: 32 (White House Collection), (detail).

Library of Congress Cataloging-in-Publication Data
Gaines, Ann.
  James K. Polk / by Ann Graham Gaines.
     p. cm. — (Presidents of the U.S.A.)
  Includes bibliographical references and index.
  ISBN 978-1-60253-040-9 (library bound : alk. paper)
 1. Polk, James K. (James Knox), 1795–1849—Juvenile literature. 2.
Presidents—United States—Biography—Juvenile literature. I. Title. II. Series.

E417.G219 2008
973.6'1092—dc22
  [B]

                              2007042611

As president, James K. Polk expanded the borders of the United States all the way to the Pacific Ocean.

TABLE OF CONTENTS

A SERIOUS BOY

James Polk was the 11th president of the United States. Although he served just one term, from 1845 to 1849, he was a very important president. The United States grew greatly in size during his presidency, expanding to reach the Pacific Ocean.

Even as a child, James Polk was a very serious person. As an adult, he was a hard worker who almost always achieved what he set out to do. And he was a man with big ideas. His drive and **determination** came from his family.

James Polk was born on November 2, 1795, in Mecklenburg County, North Carolina. He was the first child of ten children born to Samuel and Jane Polk. The Polks owned a farm. They lived in a large log cabin. They also owned at least two slaves.

James Polk was a firm believer in Manifest Destiny— the idea that the United States should expand all the way across the continent.

Samuel Polk's parents lived nearby on a bigger **plantation.** The two families spent a great deal of time together and helped each other in any way they

could. Jane and her mother-in-law canned fruits and vegetables together. Canning was a way of saving food harvested from the farm so that it could be eaten in the cold winter months. Samuel and his father, Ezekiel, helped each other harvest crops and build new barns.

James's mother went to church near their home every Sunday. James would grow up to share her belief in a stern God, who set strict rules for his people and punished sin. James Polk went to church often, but he never formally joined one.

Historians know little about James Polk's childhood. He was often ill. He had terrible pains in his stomach. In fact, he was such a sickly boy that

Polk lived in North Carolina for the first 10 years of his life. Today people can visit the site where he was born. The cabin where he lived was torn down long ago, but this one closely resembles it.

James Polk's grandfather became a hero in the American Revolution when he spiked an enemy cannon—he stuck something into it so it could not be fired anymore.

he could not attend school. His parents taught him reading, writing, and math. As a small boy, James rarely played outside. Instead, he stayed in the family's cabin with his mother. When he felt well enough, he helped do chores and took care of his younger brothers and sisters.

As a younger man, Ezekiel Polk, James's grandfather, had made many trips west into present-day Tennessee, which was wilderness land at the time. Ezekiel Polk had gone there to survey and claim land. Around 1803, after the death of his wife, Ezekiel moved to Maury County, Tennessee.

Three years later, Samuel Polk decided to move there, as well. The family, which had grown to include five children, loaded up a wagon and set out on a journey that would take six weeks. It was a hard trip.

Samuel Polk, like the pioneers shown in this illustration, packed up and moved his family from the eastern part of the country to Tennessee—which, at the time, was considered to be part of the West.

The roads were very rough. Everybody had to walk for miles and miles. They crossed wide rivers and climbed through mountain passes. As they journeyed west, the roads became little more than dusty trails. Towns became smaller and were located farther apart.

Finally, however, they arrived. The Polks settled on land that Ezekiel had bought near Nashville. They built a new cabin and barn. They had to chop down trees to clear fields and put up fences. In the years that followed, Samuel Polk bought more and more land. His small farm grew into a large plantation. He bought more slaves to work in his fields.

James Polk could not help much with the farm work because he was still sickly. He was not strong enough to work with a saw or a shovel. He also could not take part in the adventures that other frontier children enjoyed.

When James Polk was a baby, his parents took him to church for a baptism, a ceremony welcoming him into the church. When the family arrived, the minister scolded James's father because he did not attend church services each Sunday. Samuel Polk said he did not have to go to church to have faith. They argued loudly until Samuel picked up James and stormed out of the church. The ceremony never took place.

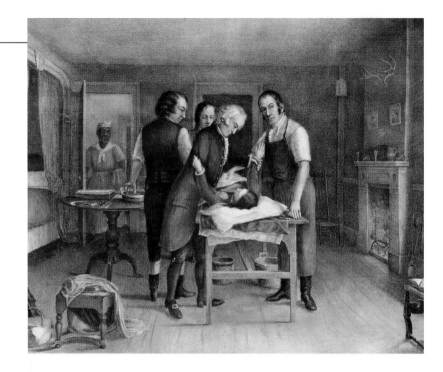

James Polk was a sickly child. When he was almost 17, he was in such pain that his parents took him to a famous surgeon who lived hundreds of miles away. Dr. Ephraim McDowell (shown here working with another patient) performed successful surgery on Polk and improved his health tremendously.

He could not often ramble through the woods or swim in cool rivers. One thing he did enjoy was horseback riding. Still, he had to spend many days in bed. Other children teased him, saying he was a weakling. This must have bothered him. By nature, he was very serious, just like his parents and grandparents.

In 1812, James Polk was often in terrible pain. His parents sent him to see a famous doctor who lived over two hundred miles away in Kentucky. Ephraim McDowell performed surgery on him, removing what historians say were urinary stones. The operation was very painful, but it was worth it! Afterward, James began to feel much better.

Back home, he went to work for a short time in a store. What he really wanted, however, was to go school.

In the summer of 1813, he enrolled in a small school started by a local minister. At that time, he was still very uneducated, having difficulty with spelling and other subjects. Yet, he learned very quickly. Soon he had learned everything he could from the minister. So he went away to live and study at a school in Murfreesboro, Tennessee. The classes he took there were more difficult. He studied Latin, Greek, literature, philosophy, math, and science.

In January 1816, James enrolled at the University of North Carolina. He rode a horse hundreds of miles from his home in Tennessee to North Carolina. There he discovered that he already knew more than many of the other students. His professors decided he could start with second-year classes. In college, he joined a **debating** club, where he learned to argue well. He developed an interest in law and government. In 1818, he graduated with honors from the university.

Biographies sometimes say that James Polk did not go to school at all while he was a child. But according to the *Tennessee Encyclopedia of History and Culture*, he did indeed go to school in Maury County from 1808 to 1810. His attendance could not have been very good, however, since he was so sickly.

Polk had attended school for only three years before he enrolled at the University of North Carolina, shown here. He graduated with top honors and then returned to Tennessee with plans to become a lawyer.

THE WEST

When James K. Polk was born, the United States was still a very young nation. At that point, most Americans lived close to the Atlantic Ocean. But as Polk grew up, more and more Americans started to head west. When Europeans first came to North America, few explored beyond the Appalachian Mountains. This rugged mountain range runs for hundreds of miles from New York south to Alabama and Georgia. It remained very hard to cross until hunters discovered the Cumberland Gap (seen above). Gaps are low places where it is easy to cross mountain ranges. Native Americans and animals had been using the Cumberland Gap for thousands of years. Once Americans found it, they began to pack their belongings and head west. The Polks were one of thousands of families that moved to Kentucky and Tennessee and lands beyond.

CHAPTER TWO

A POLITICAL CAREER

After James Polk graduated from college, he went back home to Tennessee. He had been homesick and missed his family. His father had built a fine, fancy house in the town of Columbia. By now Samuel owned thousands of acres of land and more than fifty slaves.

James Polk decided to become a lawyer. In those days, there were no special law schools. To study law, people went to work in a lawyer's office. Polk went to work in Nashville in the office of a famous attorney, Felix Grundy. He soon became interested in **politics.** In 1819, he was elected clerk of the Tennessee state senate, which met in Murfreesboro. As clerk he was something like a secretary, keeping the senate records.

In 1820, Polk passed his law exams and opened his own office in Columbia. He quickly became successful. At the same time, he led an active social life. In 1821, he met a young woman named Sarah Childress. Her father was a wealthy planter and an important man in Tennessee. Sarah was a lively, intelligent, well-educated woman. The two young people began seeing a great deal of each other.

James Polk was an ambitious and hardworking young man.

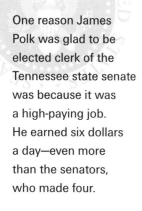

One reason James Polk was glad to be elected clerk of the Tennessee state senate was because it was a high-paying job. He earned six dollars a day—even more than the senators, who made four.

Polk continued to work as the state senate's clerk until 1822. He also developed his own political goals. Sarah Childress encouraged his growing interest in politics. Polk soon decided he wanted to run for elected office. By this time, he was a man of 27. He was serious, dedicated, and stood up for his beliefs.

In the fall of 1823, the people of Tennessee elected James Polk to their state **legislature.** He also continued to work as a lawyer. On January 1, 1824, he married Sarah Childress. Sarah delighted in his success, even though she understood he had to spend a great deal of time working, both in his law office and in the legislature. Over the years, Sarah helped James in his career. She read newspapers and documents for him. She wrote letters for him, too.

In 1825, despite the fact that he was still a young man of 30, Polk was elected to the U.S. House of Representatives, which is part of Congress. He and Sarah moved to Washington, D.C.

James Polk was a member of the Democratic Party. At that time, the U.S. president was John Quincy Adams. He belonged to the Whig Party. Polk did not like the president, his party, or his plans. Instead, he supported Andrew Jackson, another very important

Samuel Polk built this beautiful brick house in Columbia, Tennessee, while James was away at college. After he graduated, James returned to live here. He stayed with his family until he married in 1824.

political leader. Jackson was a U.S. senator. Like Polk, he was a Democrat, and he also came from Tennessee. In 1824, Jackson ran for president but lost. He would win the next election, however, and the one after that, too. Jackson was president from 1829 to 1837. During this period, he and Polk formed a friendship that lasted for life. They were political **allies.**

Sarah Childress was a bright, lively woman who had received an excellent education. She and James Polk respected each other's intelligence and shared many opinions. He trusted her completely. While Polk was president, he discussed serious issues with her. "None but Sarah," Polk once said, "knew so intimately my private affairs."

James and Sarah Polk easily settled down in the nation's busy capital city. They enjoyed life there. James liked his new job and became very active in the House of Representatives. He liked to debate important national issues of the day. He introduced many **bills,** some of which became laws. As time went by, Polk started to help Andrew Jackson. He urged other members of Congress to vote for laws the president wanted passed. In return, Jackson helped Polk meet other important **politicians.**

Tennessee's citizens reelected James Polk to the House of Representatives over and over again. In fact, he was elected seven times! Over the years, he became

In 1827, Samuel Polk died. After that, James Polk was the head of the family. When his brothers died, James helped take care of their children.

After Polk was elected to the U.S. House of Representatives, he met Andrew Jackson (right). The two men both came from Tennessee and shared many of the same beliefs. When Jackson became president in 1829, he and Polk helped each other achieve their goals.

When Polk ran for governor of Tennessee, Mrs. Polk worked to get him elected. She mailed information to voters, arranged schedules, and wrote letters.

a respected leader. He served on the very important Ways and Means Committee. This committee decides how the government should spend its money.

In 1835, James Polk took on a new responsibility when other members of Congress chose him as Speaker of the House. The Speaker takes charge of the activities in the House of Representatives. This position gave Polk a great deal of power, but he felt frustrated. He had decided that he wanted to become president one day. Although members of Congress regard the Speaker as a powerful person, most American citizens do not understand how important the position is. Polk knew the public needed to know him better before he could win a national election.

To accomplish this, Polk decided he would first try to achieve a lesser goal—to become a governor. In 1839, he left the U.S. House of Representatives and Washington, D.C. He and Sarah returned to Tennessee. They moved into a house in downtown Columbia. Within months, Polk ran for governor of Tennessee and won.

Washington, D.C., was still a rural community when the Polks moved there. They enjoyed the social life there, as well as the success that James had in his career. Even so, he decided the best way to achieve his political goals was to run for governor of his home state.

TEXAS

James Polk began serving in the U.S. Congress in 1825.
Around that time, large numbers of American settlers began
moving to Texas, which was then part of Mexico. The Mexican
government granted an American named Moses Austin a large
piece of land there. His son, Stephen, went to Texas to take
possession of the land. Soon 5,000 Americans had come to live
in the colony he established. Mexico allowed other Americans
to establish colonies in Texas, too. By 1830, 25,000 Americans
had moved there. These settlers quickly gained power in the
local governments.

Throughout Polk's term in Congress, Texas made headlines
in U.S. newspapers. At first, Americans read of the opportunities
Texas offered. There were vast spreads of open land. People

The siege of
the Alamo

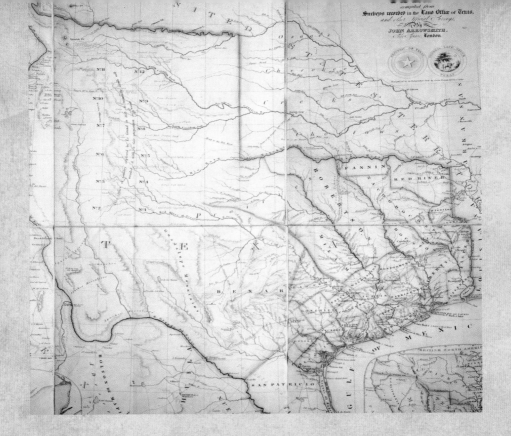

Map of the independent Republic of Texas in 1841

could build large farms for very little money. There were also rumors that silver might be found there.

In 1835, the biggest news of all arrived: Texas was on the verge of war! The Mexican government had decided it wanted more control over the American settlers who lived in Texas. The Americans did not like this.

A small group of Mexican soldiers went to Gonzales, Texas, a town settled by Americans. The soldiers demanded that the Americans return a cannon the Mexican government had given them. A battle followed that marked the beginning of what would become a revolution. The most famous battle of all took place at the Alamo. About 3,000 Mexican soldiers attacked the Texans, who were using the former mission church as a fort. For 13 days, more than 180 Texan soldiers held off their attackers. But the Mexicans finally succeeded in taking over the Alamo and killing all the Texans. At least 1,000 Mexican soldiers died in the battle as well. One month later, Texas won its independence when Texan soldiers defeated the Mexicans at the Battle of San Jacinto.

CHAPTER THREE

TEXAS AND OREGON

James Polk was elected governor of Tennessee during a difficult time, when the country was in a **depression.** As governor, he gained national attention. Polk thought that the Democratic Party might even choose him as their **candidate** for vice president in the 1840 election. This did not happen, however. The Democratic Party was in trouble. Its leaders could not agree on who should run for president. The party finally supported President Martin Van Buren for reelection, but chose no vice presidential candidate. Van Buren lost his bid for a second term.

Polk had hopes of running for vice president in 1844. Instead, he ended up being the presidential candidate.

Polk remained governor of Tennessee until 1841. He ran for reelection that year but lost. He and Sarah went home to Columbia. He wanted to run for governor again. The next election was held in 1843. Polk lost that election as well.

The next presidential election was in 1844. As it approached, Polk hoped that this time the Democrats

*Early in the 1844 presidential **campaign**, Martin Van Buren emerged as the favorite among Democratic candidates. Polk himself had campaigned for Van Buren four years before, during President Van Buren's unsuccessful 1840 bid for reelection (left). But Van Buren soon lost support because he did not want Texas to become a state. Andrew Jackson suggested that the Democrats instead **nominate** Polk as their 1844 presidential candidate.*

would ask him to run as vice president. But events took an unexpected turn. Former president Martin Van Buren wanted to run again for the job, and early on he was the favorite Democratic candidate. But ultimately, the Democrats decided they did not want Van Buren to be their candidate. This was mainly because Van Buren did not want Texas to become part of the United States. Texas had won independence from Mexico at the Battle of San Jacinto in April 1836. After the battle, Texas became an independent republic. Almost 10 years after the revolution had ended, most Texans wanted to join the United States. Many Southerners were also eager to see it join the **Union** because Texas

Polk's political friends nicknamed him Young Hickory. This was because of his friendship with Andrew Jackson, who was nicknamed Old Hickory.

This campaign poster from the 1844 election shows Democratic presidential candidate James Polk and his vice-presidential running mate George M. Dallas.

Polk was the first "dark horse" candidate. A dark horse is a candidate few people have heard of, but who wins a **political party**'s nomination.

allowed slavery. If Congress voted to admit Texas, it would mean that its members wanted slavery to remain legal in the United States.

By this time, Andrew Jackson had retired. Still, people asked for his advice. He suggested the Democrats ask James Polk to run for president. Polk had made it clear that he believed Texas should join the Union immediately. The party took Jackson's advice, and Polk agreed to seek the office.

During his presidential campaign, Polk talked about his vision: he hoped to see the country expand. He thought new land would make the United States even stronger and more powerful. He was in favor of admitting not only Texas to the Union, but the Oregon **Territory** as well.

Today Oregon is a state located north of California. In James Polk's day, a much larger area was called Oregon. From east to west, it stretched from the Rocky Mountains to the Pacific. North to south, it lay between

The Whigs made fun of Polk during his campaign. One of their campaign slogans was "Who is James K. Polk?"

A rare 1844 campaign banner with an extra star symbolizes James K. Polk's support for the admission of Texas into the Union.

the 42nd **parallel** and just over the 54th parallel at 54 degrees, 40 minutes. Degrees and minutes are measurements used to define distances. The Oregon Territory stretched from California all the way to Alaska, which then belonged to Russia.

Spanish explorers had been the first Europeans to arrive in the Oregon Territory. It was wild, wooded, and beautiful, a land **inhabited** by many Native Americans. The Spanish had claimed the territory for their king in the 1700s. In 1792, Spain gave its claim to Great Britain.

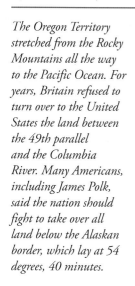

The Oregon Territory stretched from the Rocky Mountains all the way to the Pacific Ocean. For years, Britain refused to turn over to the United States the land between the 49th parallel and the Columbia River. Many Americans, including James Polk, said the nation should fight to take over all land below the Alaskan border, which lay at 54 degrees, 40 minutes.

Many animals lived in Oregon. For centuries, Native Americans had hunted otters and other creatures for food and fur. Later British and then American fur-trading companies sent traders and trappers to the area. The animal skins they trapped could be sold for a great deal of money. The region

The Oregon Territory, which included the present-day state of Oregon (above), was stunningly beautiful and rich in natural resources.

ULTIMATUM ON THE OREGON QUESTION.

The Oregon boundary dispute continued to be an issue after the 1844 election. This 1846 cartoon, written from an American perspective, supposedly shows the views of the United States (represented by Polk), Britain, and other European nations on the Oregon question. Polk is the second man from the right.

was very valuable. Both the United States and Great Britain claimed it. In 1818, a **treaty** declared that the British and Americans would share the Oregon Territory.

For many years, the United States had asked Britain to turn over all of the territory south of the 49th parallel. Britain always refused, and Americans were growing angry. During his campaign, Polk said he wanted to see Britain give up its entire claim to Oregon, not just the region below the 49th parallel. One of his campaign slogans was "Fifty-four forty or fight." This meant he believed Americans should fight to win the entire territory between California and Alaska—everything below 54 degrees, 40 minutes.

Many Americans agreed with Polk's **expansionist** views. They, too, wanted to see the nation grow larger. It was a very close election, but Polk defeated his opponent. He was on his way to the White House.

James K. Polk won the presidential election of 1844 by the smallest number of votes up until that time. More than 2.5 million men voted in the election. Polk won by just 38,000 votes.

After Polk won the presidential election, a celebratory nighttime parade was held for him in New York City.

CALIFORNIA

President Polk was determined to have the United States take control of California. He wanted this region because it held untold riches that would greatly benefit the nation.

In the 1500s, Spanish explorers became the first Europeans to see this beautiful region. They had claimed the land for their king. In 1769, Spain began to send missionaries and soldiers to build churches and forts there. They wrote letters describing the wonderful climate and how many fruits and vegetables could be grown.

Soon Great Britain, Russia, and the United States all wanted to possess California. This was not only because it could be settled and farmed, but also because there were many animals that could be trapped for fur. Captains of ships that ventured to California reported that there were many safe ports along the coast as well. In James Polk's day, the United States wanted to start trading with Asian countries such as China and Japan. Polk and other politicians realized that this would be much easier if the United States owned territory on the Pacific Ocean.

CHAPTER FOUR

PRESIDENT POLK

James Polk was at home in Columbia, Tennessee, when he received mail telling him he had been elected president of the United States. After going to celebrate the news with Andrew Jackson, James and Sarah Polk got ready to return to Washington, D.C.

James Polk was **inaugurated**—sworn into office—on March 4, 1845. He was a strong leader. During his campaign, he had promised the people that he would serve only one term as president. So he knew he had just four years to achieve the Democratic Party's four main goals. They wanted first to settle the Oregon boundary dispute. Second, they wanted to purchase California from Mexico. Third, they wanted to establish an independent **treasury,** a national department that would handle the nation's money matters. They hoped this would help cut back on the amount of money the government spent on roads, bridges, and canals. Fourth, they

Polk was 49 years old when he became president. He was the youngest president up to that time.

wanted to lower **tariffs,** which are taxes placed on goods from other countries. Lowering tariffs would make it cheaper for Americans to buy these goods.

Polk's major goal was to see the United States grow in size. Three days before Polk took office, President John Tyler had signed an act that would lead to Texas joining the United States. This meant Polk could devote his attention to other parts of the continent. Americans began to talk about Manifest Destiny, the nation's right to spread across the entire continent. Polk immediately started to plan how the U.S. could take control of Oregon and California. He felt these two western territories would bring valuable new resources to the Union. Resources are valuable things in nature, such as water or minerals.

First, Polk sent a message to Great Britain, offering to split the Oregon Territory in two. Britain would take one part of it and the United States would take the other. When the British refused his offer, the U.S. government declared it would no longer honor their agreement to share the region.

British leaders feared the United States would go to war to take over the territory. That would have cost too much money and too many lives. They finally agreed to make the 49th parallel the border between

The famous phrase "Manifest Destiny" was first used in 1845. A magazine editor used it to describe Americans' belief that the United States was destined to grow until it filled most of the North American continent.

One of the first tasks a new president faces is the selection of a cabinet. A cabinet is the group of people who help a president make important decisions. Polk (seated second from right) and his cabinet posed for this photograph in 1845. It is the oldest photograph of the White House interior known to exist.

Sarah Polk acted as an unofficial secretary and advisor for her husband during his presidency.

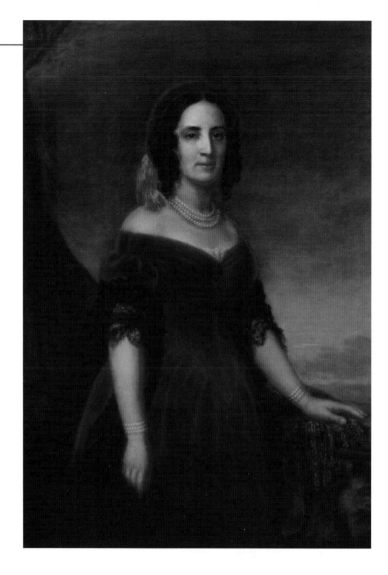

Sarah and James Polk entertained often while they lived in the White House, but they never permitted dancing or card games at their parties.

U.S. and British lands. This gave the United States what are now the states of Oregon, Washington, and Idaho. Canada, which was then a British colony, kept the land south of Alaska and north of Washington. That region is now the **province** of British Columbia. A province is a main division within Canada, much like a state in the United States.

Polk wanted the United States to grow even more. He wanted it to control California, which belonged to Mexico. He knew it was a rich land, well suited for settlement and farming. The Mexican government had been very angry when Texas joined the United States. Polk realized that Mexico would not peacefully agree to hand over California. He decided it was worth fighting for. He sent thousands of American soldiers to Texas, and they prepared to invade Mexico.

The U.S. soldiers camped along the Rio Grande River, the boundary between the United States and Mexico. President Polk wanted a war to break out, but he hoped the United States would not have to start it. He knew not all Americans supported the war. Many people in the North did not want their country to fight Mexico. They did not want the United States to add more land until Congress decided whether

Abraham Lincoln, then a young politician, opposed the Mexican War. He thought Polk and his supporters were fighting to bring more slave states into the Union.

The Polks posed for this photograph outside the White House with friends and other politicians. Barely visible at far left is another future president, James Buchanan. Second from right is Dolley Madison, the wife of the nation's fourth president, James Madison.

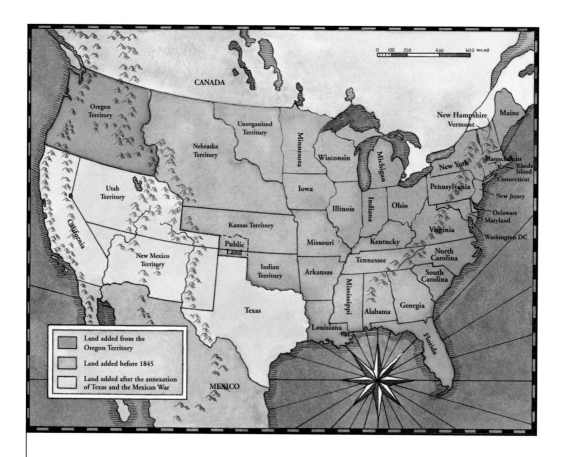

The United States grew much bigger during Polk's time in office. The yellow and green areas in the map above show land obtained during his presidency.

slavery would be legal in new states. People also complained because the war would cost money, and too many soldiers would lose their lives. Polk hoped that Mexico would either accept a U.S. offer to buy California or be so angry at the presence of an American army on its border that it would fight to drive it away. Then he could tell the American people he had no choice but to order the American army to fight back.

For a long time, Mexico failed to attack. Polk thought the United States might have to start the war. But finally Mexican troops crossed the Rio Grande River and captured American soldiers. Congress declared war on Mexico in May of 1846, just as the president had wanted.

The Mexican War continued for a year and a half. The American army invaded Mexico and won many victories. Finally, it **occupied** the capital, Mexico City. Mexico then had to give in to the United States. In 1848, Mexico agreed to the Treaty of Guadalupe Hidalgo, which gave the United States land that would become the states of Arizona, Nevada, California, Utah, and parts of New Mexico, Colorado, and Wyoming. The treaty added nearly 1.2 million square miles to the Union. Polk regarded this as his greatest achievement. Americans also praised him at the war's end.

The very year that California became part of the United States, gold was discovered there. The news traveled by ship to the eastern United States. One of the first shipments of gold nuggets was sent to President Polk. In the years that followed, Americans,

Three states were added to the Union during Polk's presidency: Iowa, Wisconsin, and Texas. Many other states would later be created out of land acquired during Polk's presidency. They included Washington, Oregon, Idaho, Arizona, Nevada, California, and Utah. In the Mexican War, the United States also won parts of what would be New Mexico, Colorado, and Wyoming.

Toward the end of Polk's presidency, people began journeying to one of the nation's newest territories, California. They hoped to strike it rich, for gold had just been discovered there. The Gold Rush would continue for many years, as people traveled to California dreaming of a new life.

In 1995, the U.S. government celebrated the 200th anniversary of James Polk's birth by issuing a postage stamp in his honor.

As he had promised, Polk did not run for reelection in 1848. He was tired and ready to give up the great responsibilities of the presidency.

as well as people from many other countries, flocked to California. They hoped to strike it rich.

When he ran for president in 1844, Polk had promised he would serve only one term as president. He kept this promise. He was very popular at the end of the war, but he did not run for reelection in 1848. Tired and ill, Polk was ready to leave the task of running the nation to someone else. Just before he left office, Polk wrote about his time as president: "They have been four years of . . . labor and anxiety. I am heartily rejoiced that my term is so near its close." A hero named Zachary Taylor had gained fame as a general during the Mexican War. He was elected president and took office in 1849.

After Taylor's inauguration, the Polks returned to Tennessee. James Polk was tired. He had been working too hard for a long time. He had never taken a single day of vacation. A lack of rest had left him weak. Just three months after his return home, he became sick with **cholera.** His exhausted body could not fight off his illness. He died just three months after returning to Tennessee, at the age of 53.

James Polk had been a hardworking and determined man. As president, he had fulfilled his great goal, helping the country grow much larger in size. His vision and strength allowed the United States to stretch across the continent.

THE MEXICAN WAR

About 100,000 American soldiers fought in the Mexican War. Although fewer than 2,000 of them died in battle, the war was terrible for all. It began on the Rio Grande, the river on the border between Texas and Mexico. In battle after battle, the American troops were outnumbered. Most of these battles took place on Mexican soil, which gave the enemy an advantage. The U.S. Navy carried some soldiers to Mexico on boats. But most marched hundreds of miles across hot, dry deserts.

In those days, soldiers still fought with swords as well as guns. Battles could be very bloody. American soldiers also suffered from serious diseases. More than 11,000 men died from disease—many more than died in battle. Soldiers' families knew the real cost of the war. Even so, most Americans rejoiced over the victory. The United States gained 1.2 million square miles of land at the war's end.

TIME LINE

1795
James Polk is born on November 2 in North Carolina.

1806
The Polk family moves to Tennessee.

1812
Polk undergoes a dangerous operation. After he recovers, he is healthy enough to go to school.

1816
Polk enrolls at the University of North Carolina.

1818
Polk graduates from college after just two years of study. He returns home to Tennessee where he studies law with a well-known lawyer.

1819
Polk takes a job as clerk to the Tennessee State Senate.

1820
Polk finishes his law studies. He becomes a lawyer and opens his own law office in Columbia, Tennessee.

1821
Polk begins to court Sarah Childress.

1822
Polk resigns his position as clerk for the state senate.

1823
Polk is elected to the Tennessee state legislature.

1824
Polk marries Sarah Childress.

1825
Polk is elected to the U.S. House of Representatives. He and Sarah Polk move to Washington, D.C.

1827
Polk is reelected to the House. He goes on to be reelected five more times.

1828
Andrew Jackson is elected president. Polk and Jackson become political allies. Over the years, Jackson helps Polk meet important politicians. Polk helps Jackson pass bills in the House.

1835
Members of Congress elect Polk to the important position of Speaker of the House.

1836
After the Texans win their independence from Mexico, they establish the Republic of Texas, an independent nation.

1837
Martin Van Buren is inaugurated president on March 4.

1839
Polk leaves the House of Representatives. He and Sarah return to Tennessee, where he is elected governor.

1840
The Democratic candidate, President Martin Van Buren, loses the presidential election to Whig candidate William Henry Harrison.

1841
Polk runs for reelection as governor of Tennessee, but loses. President Harrison dies after only one month in office. His vice president, John Tyler, becomes president.

1843
Polk runs for election as governor of Tennessee, but loses once again.

1844
The Democratic Party, in a surprise move, nominates Polk as its presidential candidate. During the campaign, he supports the expansion of the United States into the West. He promises to support the annexation of Texas. He wins the election.

1845
Polk is inaugurated on March 4. He immediately begins to negotiate with Great Britain for the Oregon Territory. The independent republic of Texas agrees to join the Union in July and officially becomes a state in December. The United States fights with Mexico over the southern border of Texas.

1846
Great Britain agrees to turn over to the United States all land south of the 49th parallel in the Oregon Territory. In May, the Mexican War begins. Earlier, Polk had sent U.S. soldiers to Texas, hoping for war to break out. He hopes to win Mexico's rich land in California.

1847
Americans capture Mexico City, which will end the Mexican War.

1848
In late January, gold is discovered in California. In February, the Treaty of Guadalupe Hidalgo with Mexico gives the United States nearly 1.2 million square miles of western land and firmly establishes the border between Mexico and Texas. Polk decides not to run for a second term as president. War hero Zachary Taylor is elected president in the November election. In December, Polk receives a package containing gold nuggets from California.

1849
When the news of gold in California spreads, the Gold Rush begins. Zachary Taylor is inaugurated president in March. James and Sarah Polk return home to Tennessee. James Polk dies there on June 15, at the age of 53.

GLOSSARY

allies (AL-lize) Allies are people or groups of people who help each other by working toward a common goal. Jackson and Polk were political allies.

bills (BILZ) Bills are ideas for new laws that are presented to a group of lawmakers. Polk introduced many bills to the House of Representatives.

campaign (kam-PAYN) A campaign is the process of running for an election, including activities such as giving speeches or attending rallies. Polk focused on expansionism during his campaign.

candidate (KAN-dih-det) A candidate is a person running in an election. Polk hoped the Democratic Party would choose him as its candidate for vice president in 1840.

cholera (KOL-ur-uh) Cholera is a dangerous disease that causes severe illness and diarrhea. James Polk died of cholera.

debating (dih-BAY-ting) Debating is the discussion of a question or topic, considering reasons for and against it. Polk joined a debating club in college.

depression (di-PRESH-uhn) A depression is a time when businesses aren't doing well and many people become poor. When Polk was governor of Tennessee, the nation was in a depression.

determination (di-tur-min-AY-shun) Determination is the act of deciding definitely and firmly to do something. James Polk possessed the quality of determination.

expansionist (ek-SPAN-shun-ist) An expansionist is a person who wants to increase the size of something. Polk was an expansionist because he wanted the United States to grow.

historians (hih-STOR-ee-unz) Historians are people who are experts in history. Historians do not know very much about Polk's childhood.

inaugurated (ih-NAWG-yur-ay-ted) Inaugurated means sworn into office. Polk was inaugurated as president on March 4, 1845.

inhabited (in-HAB-ih-tid) If you inhabit a place, you live there. The Oregon Territory was inhabited by many Native Americans.

legislature (LEJ-uh-slay-chur) A legislature is the part of a government that makes laws. Polk was elected to the Tennessee state legislature in 1823.

Manifest Destiny (MAN-uh-fest DES-tuh-nee) Manifest Destiny was a belief in the early 1800s that the United States had a right to expand across the entire continent.

nominate (NOM-ih-nayt) If a political party nominates someone, it chooses him or her to run for a political office. The Democrats nominated Martin Van Buren as their presidential candidate in 1840.

occupied (AHK-yeh-pyd) If a place has been occupied, it has been taken over by force. American soldiers occupied Mexico City during the Mexican War.

parallel (PAYR-uh-lel) A parallel is an imaginary line that circles the Earth and is used on maps and globes for measurement. The parallels are equal spaces apart from each other and measure distance from the equator.

plantation (plan-TAY-shun) A plantation is a large farm or group of farms that grows crops such as tobacco, sugarcane, or cotton. The Polks' small farm grew into a large plantation.

political party (puh-LIT-uh-kul PAR-tee) A political party is a group of people who share similar ideas about how to run a government. Polk was a member of the Democratic political party.

politicians (pawl-ih-TISH-unz) Politicians are people who hold public office. Polk met other politicians when he began his career in politics.

politics (PAWL-uh-tiks) Politics refers to the actions and practices of the government. Polk became interested in politics while he was studying to become a lawyer.

province (PROV-uhnss) A province is a district or region of some countries. Canada is divided into provinces.

republic (ree-PUB-lik) A republic is a nation with a government elected by its citizens. Texas was an independent republic after the Texas Revolution.

revolution (rev-uh-LOO-shun) A revolution is something that causes a complete change in government. Texas fought a revolution to win its independence from Mexico in 1836.

tariffs (TAR-iffs) Tariffs are taxes on foreign goods. During Polk's presidency, the Democratic Party wanted to lower tariffs so Americans could buy foreign goods more cheaply.

territory (TAYR-uh-tor-ee) A territory is a land or region, especially land that belongs to a government. Polk wanted the Oregon Territory to become part of the United States.

treasury (TREZH-uhr-ee) A treasury manages a government's money, including its income and expenses. The Democratic Party wanted Polk to establish a national treasury.

treaty (TREE-tee) A treaty is a formal agreement between nations. In 1818, a treaty declared that the British and Americans would share the Oregon Territory.

union (YOON-yen) A union is the joining together of two people or groups of people, such as states. The Union is another name for the United States.

THE UNITED STATES GOVERNMENT

The United States government is divided into three equal branches: the executive, the legislative, and the judicial. This division helps prevent abuses of power because each branch has to answer to the other two. No one branch can become too powerful.

EXECUTIVE BRANCH

PRESIDENT
VICE PRESIDENT
DEPARTMENTS

The job of the executive branch is to enforce the laws. It is headed by the president, who serves as the spokesperson for the United States around the world. The president signs bills into law and appoints important officials such as federal judges. He or she is also the commander in chief of the U.S. military. The president is assisted by the vice president, who takes over if the president dies or cannot carry out the duties of the office.

The executive branch also includes various departments, each focused on a specific topic. They include the Defense Department, the Justice Department, and the Agriculture Department. The department heads, along with other officials such as the vice president, serve as the president's closest advisers, called the cabinet.

LEGISLATIVE BRANCH

CONGRESS
Senate and
House of Representatives

The job of the legislative branch is to make the laws. It consists of Congress, which is divided into two parts: the Senate and the House of Representatives. The Senate has 100 members, and the House of Representatives has 435 members. Each state has two senators. The number of representatives a state has varies depending on the state's population.

Besides making laws, Congress also passes budgets and enacts taxes. In addition, it is responsible for declaring war, maintaining the military, and regulating trade with other countries.

JUDICIAL BRANCH

SUPREME COURT
COURTS OF APPEALS
DISTRICT COURTS

The job of the judicial branch is to interpret the laws. It consists of the nation's federal courts. Trials are held in district courts. During trials, judges must decide what laws mean and how they apply. Courts of appeals review the decisions made in district courts.

The nation's highest court is the Supreme Court. If someone disagrees with a court of appeals ruling, he or she can ask the Supreme Court to review it. The Supreme Court may refuse. The Supreme Court makes sure that decisions and laws do not violate the Constitution.

CHOOSING THE PRESIDENT

It may seem odd, but American voters don't elect the president directly. Instead, the president is chosen using what is called the Electoral College.

Each state gets as many votes in the Electoral College as its combined total of senators and representatives in Congress. For example, Iowa has two senators and five representatives, so it gets seven electoral votes. Although the District of Columbia does not have any voting members in Congress, it gets three electoral votes. Usually, the candidate who wins the most votes in any given state receives all of that state's electoral votes.

To become president, a candidate must get more than half of the Electoral College votes. There are a total of 538 votes in the Electoral College, so a candidate needs 270 votes to win. If nobody receives 270 Electoral College votes, the House of Representatives chooses the president.

With the Electoral College system, the person who receives the most votes nationwide does not always receive the most electoral votes. This happened most recently in 2000, when Al Gore received half a million more national votes than George W. Bush. Bush became president because he had more Electoral College votes.

THE WHITE HOUSE

The White House is the official home of the president of the United States. It is located at 1600 Pennsylvania Avenue NW in Washington, D.C. In 1792, a contest was held to select the architect who would design the president's home. James Hoban won. Construction took eight years.

The first president, George Washington, never lived in the White House. The second president, John Adams, moved into the house in 1800, though the inside was not yet complete. During the War of 1812, British soldiers burned down much of the White House. It was rebuilt several years later.

The White House was changed through the years. Porches were added, and President Theodore Roosevelt added the West Wing. President William Taft changed the shape of the presidential office, making it into the famous Oval Office. While Harry Truman was president, the old house was discovered to be structurally weak. All the walls were reinforced with steel, and the rooms were rebuilt.

Today, the White House has 132 rooms (including 35 bathrooms), 28 fireplaces, and 3 elevators. It takes 570 gallons of paint to cover the outside of the six-story building. The White House provides the president with many ways to relax. It includes a putting green, a jogging track, a swimming pool, a tennis court, and beautifully landscaped gardens. The White House also has a movie theater, a billiard room, and a one-lane bowling alley.

PRESIDENTIAL PERKS

The job of president of the United States is challenging. It is probably one of the most stressful jobs in the world. Because of this, presidents are paid well, though not nearly as well as the leaders of large corporations. In 2007, the president earned $400,000 a year. Presidents also receive extra benefits that make the demanding job a little more appealing.

★ **Camp David:** In the 1940s, President Franklin D. Roosevelt chose this heavily wooded spot in the mountains of Maryland to be the presidential retreat, where presidents can relax. Even though it is a retreat, world business is conducted there. Most famously, President Jimmy Carter met with Middle Eastern leaders at Camp David in 1978. The result was a peace agreement between Israel and Egypt.

★ *Air Force One*: The president flies on a jet called *Air Force One*. It is a Boeing 747-200B that has been modified to meet the president's needs.

Air Force One is the size of a large home. It is equipped with a dining room, sleeping quarters, a conference room, and office space. It also has two kitchens that can provide food for up to 50 people.

★ **The Secret Service:** While not the most glamorous of the president's perks, the Secret Service is one of the most important. The Secret Service is a group of highly trained agents who protect the president and the president's family.

★ **The Presidential State Car:** The presidential limousine is a stretch Cadillac DTS.

It has been armored to protect the president in case of attack. Inside the plush car are a foldaway desk, an entertainment center, and a communications console.

★ **The Food:** The White House has five chefs who will make any food the president wants. The White House also has an extensive wine collection.

★ **Retirement:** A former president receives a pension, or retirement pay, of just under $180,000 a year. Former presidents also receive Secret Service protection for the rest of their lives.

FACTS

QUALIFICATIONS

To run for president, a candidate must

- ★ be at least 35 years old
- ★ be a citizen who was born in the United States
- ★ have lived in the United States for 14 years

TERM OF OFFICE

A president's term of office is four years.
No president can stay in office for more than two terms.

ELECTION DATE

The presidential election takes place every four years on the first Tuesday of November.

INAUGURATION DATE

Presidents are inaugurated on January 20.

OATH OF OFFICE

I do solemnly swear I will faithfully execute the office of the President of the United States and will to the best of my ability preserve, protect, and defend the Constitution of the United States.

WRITE A LETTER TO THE PRESIDENT

One of the best things about being a U.S. citizen is that Americans get to participate in their government. They can speak out if they feel government leaders aren't doing their jobs. They can also praise leaders who are going the extra mile. Do you have something you'd like the president to do? Should the president worry more about the environment and encourage people to recycle? Should the government spend more money on our schools? You can write a letter to the president to say how you feel!

1600 Pennsylvania Avenue
Washington, D.C. 20500
You can even send an e-mail to: president@whitehouse.gov

BOOKS

Bardhan-Quallen, Sudipta. *The Mexican-American War.*
Detroit: Blackbird Press, 2005.

Behrman, Carol H. *James K. Polk.* Minneapolis: Lerner
Publishing Company, 2005.

Boekhoff, P. M., and Stuart A. Kallen. *Oregon.* San Diego:
Kidhaven Press, 2004.

Carey Jr., Charles W. *The Mexican War: "Mr Polk's War."*
Berkeley Heights, N.J.: Enslow, 2002.

Sinnott, Susan. *Sarah Childress Polk, 1803–1891.* New
York: Children's Press, 1998.

VIDEOS

The American President. DVD, VHS (Alexandria, VA: PBS
Home Video, 2000).

The History Channel Presents The Presidents. DVD (New
York: A & E Home Video, 2005).

National Geographic's Inside the White House. DVD
(Washington, D.C.: National Geographic Video, 2003).

U.S. Mexican War, 1846–1848. The Hour of Sacrifice. VHS
(Alexandria, VA: PBS Home Video, 1998).

INTERNET SITES

Visit our Web page for lots of links about
James K. Polk and other U.S. presidents:

http://www.childsworld.com/links

Note to Parents, Teachers, and Librarians: We routinely verify our Web links to make
sure they are safe, active sites—so encourage your readers to check them out!

INDEX